88 MAPS

88 MAPS

poems Rob Carney

LOST HORSE PRESS
Sandpoint, Idaho

Cover Art: A Multiverse Explanation by Rune Guneriussen. www.runeguneriussen.no
Book & Cover Design: Christine Holbert.

FIRST EDITION

This and other fine LOST HORSE PRESS titles may be viewed online at
www.losthorsepress.org.

LIBRARY OF CONGRESS CATALOGING-IN-PUBLICATION DATA

Carney, Rob, 1968-
[Poems. Selections] 88 maps : poems / by Rob Carney.—First edition.
     pages cm
ISBN 978-0-9908193-3-2 (alk. paper)
I. Title. II. Title: Eighty-eight maps.
PS3603.A7653A6 2015
811'.6—dc23
                          2015024042

CONTENTS

I

DEPARTURES

88 Maps

I found them rolled up, dusty, in an old armoire
too big to get out of the cellar—

no way to fit it through the door frame
and angle it up the stairwell—

decades ago he must have hauled down wood
and built it where it stands.

And it's not just a place to store winter jackets.
He was being deliberately permanent,

sawing, planing, and jointing
more than six feet underground.

•

In one he's mapped the yard's topography,
detailing valleys and elevations:

the small concavity above his cat's bones
where loosened dirt

sunk slowly in the rain,
the spire of the mailbox,

each scattered rock in the flower garden.
And somehow the scent of the peach tree. Above that,

each jut of the roof line. And higher still,
his back-porch view of the craters on the moon.

·

I've studied them all,
even hung some in picture frames:

Pathways of Wind 'Round the Kitchen,
Locations of Dishes and Silverware,

A Chronological Survey of Fire
from Timber Harvest to December Snow

with an inset map of newspaper catching,
then kindling and logs, then a dance of shadows

like a man and a woman lost in bodies . . .
then the long glow of coals,

·

though not as long as hate, and he mapped that too:
a stack of false starts crossed out.

Unless false starts *are* the landscape.
And those Xs represent years.

·

There's no way to know what he meant,
or why he built this atlas of routine:

tidal charts of his room-to-room movements,
the constellations of upstairs furniture,

mechanical drawings of going to buy more milk.
But he painted an eighth great continent,

and the name in its center is *Baby,*
and sometimes saying that word aloud,

I feel its weight.
Like a mountain range, or bird.

.

He made a color wheel of history
according to the trees—

brown, green, blossom colors,
more green, oranges, brown—

and a globe from the point of view of hummingbirds,
small as a flower.

He made a cylinder cut-out for player piano,
claiming to recreate finch songs.

He made a scale to measure the impact
of slamming doors.

None of them maps, exactly,
not even his *Diagram for Boxes:*

a set of illustrations and arrows
with instructions on how to unfold.

·

Why the people who sold me this house didn't want them,
I can't say.

Maybe they knew where they were going.
Maybe maps with no recognized compass

can't point the way,
at least not in straight lines. . . .

And they left me some half-full paint cans, an ant trap
under the refrigerator,

and a map of the Salt Lake metro area
in case I'd moved from out of state,

•

which I *have* used once: on a wasp in the window.
It was the nearest thing at hand.

•

Eighty-eight maps—
I know 'cause I've counted—

the exact same number as keys on a piano,
and maybe if you laid them out side by side

they'd play a song,
though of course that's impossible—

they're just maps. They're not magic.
Years ago, somebody made them . . .

a man who never signed his work,
so I don't know his name.

•

I know about maps, though:
the way they all start somewhere,

how they picture the in-between rises
and valleys—

the roof lines and kindling
and armoires and cats' bones—

but always arrive at the ocean, stars, or underground
whichever way we go.

II

DIRECTIONS

Here in the Rugged, Noble West,

it's legislative season, and guys in ties and shoe shines are worried about wolves, concocting *Wolf Management Plans*. So here's mine:

1. If a wolf pack kills a cow, all senators go without a burger.

2. The rancher and his family get a free trip to Norway to ski or sail the fjords.

3. If a hunter goes without a trophy elk, he gets a half an hour of my sympathy.

4. If wolves lope into your dreams, you have my praise. I wish I could be there too—the snow done falling, the wind stopped still in its tracks, all of us waiting.

5. If they circle inside you like a hungry idea, it's a sign that you're unfit for office.

6. At random places on the interstate, I'll post arrows pointing out the moon.

If Wolves Lope into Your Dreams,

they're a sign that something's coming,
a message you need to be still inside to hear.

And it won't be a woman's name,
though some have names like music.

And it won't be a woman's body,
though some are shaped like music. No,

they'll draw a wide circle around your disquiet
and howl . . . the opposite of avenues,

the opposite of the neighbors' backyard dog
barking in time with your heartbeat. . . .

Right now a wolf is dreaming too,
and it isn't dreaming of people.

Behind its eyes, it's chasing the mountains,
wanting to tear the Earth from its hold on the moon.

Eagle Ridge, Eagle Crest, Eagle View

Away from the city, there are still some fields
tucked behind houses on the outskirts,

houses a bit like museums
since a few have barns and the rare noise of roosters.

Dump trucks are busy nearby, churning dust clouds,
and shovel-headed cranes—each great bite of dirt

another inch of road,
another new customer.

Meanwhile, the wind is busy with its own work,
bending the trees back like dancers,

and nine crows ride on the updraft in a line.
I'm not a pioneer either, but I can read this weather:

It won't be long before these pastures
are a memory,

and somewhere on one of these remnant acres,
somebody's spring calf is dead.

Every Place I've Ever Lived Is Gone:

pecan groves outside of Lafayette,
the pine woods north of Spokane,

the field by my house where the snow piled deep,
where a snow owl passed so silently and low

it changed my idea of ghosts —
now they're stores,

and neighborhoods named after trees,
and spillover parking for a church,

and maybe the choir sings hymns so beautifully
it's fine; I'll call it the future, agree that it's bright.

But west of Washtucna, Washington,
the highway stretches through the dark . . .

miles of no-place, of in-between,
that haven't disappeared.

Freight trucks are too few to bother me much,
and wind off the river cools the hood down.

I can stop on the shoulder and sit there still
while stars fill every inch of night.

Suggestions for Urban Renewal:

1. A No Umbrellas ordinance. Instead of poking holes in the rain, people would have to wear hats.

2. Let's take away hats while we're at it, make everyone risk being sexy. A woman with gray-sky eyes, for instance . . . hair darker, the ends of it curling.

3. One rainy day on Grafton Street, I waited out the weather drinking tea. This was Dublin, so I needed a second pot. Then a third with a girl who'd noticed my accent.

4. A short walk from there to the National Gallery. We outran the next burst of rain: Kandinsky, Chagall, of course . . . the Renaissance in marble . . . and her face still flushed from the cold and the running . . . a drop she hadn't yet blinked from her lashes . . .

5. then she showed me—I didn't even know he had a brother—a room full of paintings by Jack Yeats.

6. They were amazing,

7. like rain at night on a metal roof. Or watching a storm from a wide front porch. Or

8. maybe just red umbrellas, some color to contrast the overcast.

9. A retail anchor's not the answer.

10. A new Target's not where people fall in love.

"Break a Leg, and They Put You Out to Pasture"

Processional

"Take everything you don't know, line it up,
you've got the horizon. But get your head in a book,

you've got a boat." That's the kind of thing he'll say
between two bites of an apple.

It's one of the reasons I don't mind him crossing the street
when I'm watering the yard.

He's earned these analogies:
worked twenty-three years as a fire jumper,

wound up with seven breaks in his ankle and leg,
a whole scaffolding of steel inside.

Another reason is the cider he brings me—
"Easiest way to deal with the apples."

He says, "I ought to just burn the damn tree,
but I'm too used to putting fires out."

Arrival

"Maybe not a boat, exactly. But an oar, for sure.
Or a spyglass." By now he's wielding the hose

while I follow and watch,
fake professional interest.

He's spraying at the bees around the flowers
like he's putting out sparks.

He's probably right about the spyglass: You open a book
and draw the distance nearer,

the words inside it help clarify,
and it's all done with mirrors, by reflection. Not a bad trick.

It makes me wonder sometimes
if a tree he saved became paper . . .

or a hundred board feet of pencils . . .
or a chair in a bookstore café.

Burial

I imagine the heat, of course—
everywhere-pressing and heavy as water—

but the roar of standing in a world of fire,
not a pulsing and pausing like the shoreline's heartbeat,

a constant sound
swallowing all sound, that's harder to do.

And thirst. I half forgot about thirst:
all those back-to-back shifts drinking nothing but smoke.

"I could've retired," he says.
"No one expects more than twenty.

But it felt like jumping into empty air
and then landing with nothing to do."

The hose is rolled up by the side of the house now,
the whole yard shining from sunlight on water,

and we're standing on the porch, drinking cider,
talking about raccoons.

They're his only regret, he tells me. Not the leg;
he's seen tree trunks more shattered.

Four baby raccoons, maybe five months old.
He saw the flames reflecting off their eyes,

pulled them out of a hollow, shoved them in his coat,
got them down to the base camp,

poured iodine onto the bite marks and scratches,
went back in.

He found out the next morning.
"They just took 'em to the county pound and put 'em to sleep."

Recessional

There's a field I pass by on my way to work
so out of place in the landscape —

too close to new tract homes and cul-de-sacs, shopping,
a thousand miles from Texas, a hitch

in the step, a break in the usual line —
where they're grazing all these longhorn cows.

I love that part of the drive. I don't belong here either.
My neighbor and I, we've got that in common,

enough that we never have to talk about it,
enough we just wave in the winter

while shoveling snow, unburying sidewalks.
It's how I know that he really will burn that tree,

yell out at me to come on over. . . .
He'll hand me a last jar of cider,

then stand there, probably with pain in his leg.
And I'll stand there too and help him watch the fire.

Here in What Used to Be Mexico,

it's legislative season, and guys in invisible Stetsons are worried about me if my name were Hernandez. They want plans for an immigration round-up, so here's mine:

1. No "illegals," and no "anchor babies"; *no mas*. From now on counterfeiting words is a punishable crime.

2. Our language is a language not a lug nut,

3. and you're a thinking human being not a wrench.

4. An immigrant standing on a New York girder looked up at what they were building. Eleven men, boots dangling, put their lunches down when they heard him. He said, "We should call this a 'skyscraper'." And we do.

5. If they live in your thoughts like a hungry idea, you might ask if some of them are hungry.

6. I'll keep on tipping at the taco cart. *"Tres con barbacoa, por favor."*

To the Man in the Jaunty Golf Cap, Wow—

I'm glad that wool was saved from coyotes,
glad for winter with its sight lines, glad for trees,

the way they cooperate
by letting go of their leaves.

And I'm glad for the skill of the helicopter pilot,
ski-smooth even in the crosswinds,

glad for rifles and marksmanship: one coyote less, gone
before the gunshot echo. . . .

Even from the air, even over naked snow,
I'd never see so clearly,

see tracks as a map they can't run away from, tracks
just one step behind,

but it isn't my job.
It isn't the clouds' job either,

topping the mountains like a jaunty hat.
Theirs is to part and let the sunlight accent

the quiet on the green, and you there
lining up a putt.

To the Man Who Scored 300k to Cry Wolf Before Congress on Behalf of Utah, a State in Which There Are No Wolves,*

I picture it like this: You order elk,
wild mushrooms, on a bed of rice—wild rice,

and cunning, vicious. Rice you have to stalk
across the tundra, the inhospitable ice,

loping on snowshoes . . . that can't be easy.
Rice you bring down and haul back to D.C.

I hope our state appreciates your work
to block wolf packs' access, every dessert

you're willing to risk—pear amandines in spun
honey, sorbet with a cherry reduction—

each Johnnie Walker Blue for each congressman.
Cheers. The least we owe you is a sonnet.

And a three-hundred-thousand-dollar budget
like a bag of charms to keep the absent wolves away.

*Big Game Forever—basically an anti-wolf lobbying group consisting of a guy named Don Peay—got this line-item spending during the 2013 legislative session. Brian Maffly's story in *The Salt Lake Tribune* (March 7, 2013) details it nicely.

To the Representative on the House Science, Space, and Technology Committee, Who in 2012 Said, "Evolution, Big Bang Theory, All That Is Lies Straight from the Pit of Hell,"* I Offer This Quick Study on Natural Selection, in Which the Eagle Is Thought; the River Is Reason; the Salmon Is Insight; Tomorrow Is a Salmon; and the Crows, of Course, Are You

No one sees the end when they begin:
not the eagle letting go and going back

to catch another fish, not the snow pack
becoming this river, not the salmon

yanked from the water, not even the crows—
that cawing hassle, mob of black

harassing the eagle. We never see the end
because of hope.

But that salmon didn't make it home to spawn.
The eagle's flown downstream and out of view

beyond a river bend. The afternoon's moved on
toward tomorrow, and tomorrow is a fish,

another occasion, like all these crows, to turn and argue . . .
or not. I'll throw coins in the river, make a wish.

*His name is Paul Broun, and his speech did get him in the news. See, for instance, Matt Pearce's article in the October 7, 2012, *Los Angeles Times*.

To the Woman at the Conference on Writing for Social Change Who Asked, "What Was Your Upbringing? What Were Your Parents Like? How Did You Get This Open-minded?" . . . I Don't Remember My Answer but Wish I'd Said This:

I grew up in a neighborhood of rain and trees.
My mom and dad were teachers.

Sometimes they drove us to the shoreline
and let me drag kelp, climb driftwood,

think wind and waves
were the Earth's conversation.

Because of them, I eat king crab and salmon.
Because of them, I love mussels and clams,

love the pile-up of emptying blue shells
and white shells, and the flavors of ocean with beer.

•

One time after some grumbling of mine,
a complaint taking longer than it needed to,

my grandma said, "Yes, a few do the carrying
for the rest. Now which would you rather be?"

She never was tall to begin with
before age and osteoporosis did their number.

Things like that, though, showed me
she only *looked* small.

·

On the school bus after an all-night storm, passing
the mud of an undone pasture

and cows still packed together in the middle,
a huddle of soaked hides and windblown . . .

passing through a moment of their animal lives
on our way to second grade, my friend said, "Cows—

they just have to stand there.
Think about it."

And I do.
He saw more than I did that morning.

·

Even you. Your question.
For two days I've kept trying to answer:

in my head in the car on the way to work . . .
last night rinsing the dishes.

But my thoughts can't total it up yet
except to say thanks,

thanks for calling my poems open-minded.
That seems a good measure to go by. I won't forget.

The Church of the Stars and the Moon

Processional

Of course they weren't resurrecting.
But the mouse I found in the garden one evening—

dropped by the carrots when my cat got bored—
and the dead bird, broken, in the deck chair—

such a nice spot to stretch out easy while you're thinking,
while you're pinning one wing

and watching the other one flail—
in the morning, when I went back to toss them,

they were gone.
And then I could hear it for certain:

a call that wasn't like *Hooo*
but more like *More-more.*

Arrival

And so I had an owl,
a little piece of neighborhood lightning.

I'd swing by the pet store,
buy mice to stock the yard,

and keep watch,
my eyes tuned to shadows.

I'd will the street to sit still and be quiet
so the owl would let go and glide,

carve its arc across the backyard darkness,
just a hitch—one moment—

when the talons clutched,
then gone,

the best part of summer.
I only saw it once.

Burial

But I found where the bones wound up:
always at the base of a telephone pole

in the alley behind the garage.
I noticed ants one day in their organized scramble—

sure enough:
an above-ground catacomb,

a toss of miniature driftwood,
deposit of *dead*.

It probably liked the crossbeam—
like a long, high table with an open view of below—

and ate unhurried,
and ate well,

then sat like a messenger angel
in The Church of the Stars and the Moon.

Don't believe it's impossible.
If angels are real, then an angel might be an owl.

Recessional

They do seem to be intercessors,
calling out across the empty spaces,

their gold eyes filling up zeroes,
their wings like a bridge, something reaching

from up to down, lower to higher,
at least for a while.

I miss my owl's company.
I wish it had stayed all summer.

But maybe, like angels, they belong to no one.
Maybe wildness is an answer from the sky.

III

NO RETURN ADDRESS

Undercurrents

Seems like every weekend in the summer here, someone wants to take you down to Moab. You go there and hang out and marvel at nature and beauty. Like it's your job. Sure, there's the Colorado River, but growing up in Washington, we had rivers too. Greg and I and some other friends in high school, we used to go tubing every chance we got: five-foot waterfalls, and fallen trees you had to flatten out to duck under, and it was *really* fast one time — they'd opened the flood gates; we found out later on the news — and we could hear these rapids coming up . . . water so strong it yanked my shorts off . . . and on the last drop there's this boulder underwater, and *Bam!* . . . I couldn't ride my bike for a month. It could've been worse, though. Somebody died that day. Drowned. One of our moms — probably mine; she's always been a worrier — anyway, one of our moms filled us in on the details as soon as we got home. . . . What's it been now, twenty years? But once in a while it comes back to me, how this guy went out and drowned, and he *didn't* come back, and all the people who knew him . . . I mean, somebody had to — he could've had a girlfriend, parents, a kid sister or brother, how should I know? — what I'm saying is there must be someone who's still sick about that summer because this guy they loved went out and ended up dead. No more telling him it's time for dinner. No more sex or calling him on the telephone. Gone. Just memories. And even those getting less and less every year. . . . It's pretty weird when you think about it: The things I remember about that day are mostly good. My friends and I, we all had a great time.

Lost and Found

Greg's got a cabin up in Priest lake, Idaho. He built the boat dock himself. He said his dad was never prouder. I'm not saying it's a fishing lodge or anything, but it's nice. It's a lot better than a lot of cabins, that's for sure. Like the one he had in Alaska when he was working for Fish and Game: a worn out A-frame not much bigger than a teepee. No foundation under it—you can't do that on permafrost—so it was propped up on blocks, and any clothes he wasn't wearing he'd spread on the floor, trying to keep the wind from coming through the cracks. He said it had a stove like a fire-breathing dragon. Dangerous. And an outhouse, no bathroom; winters are too cold for plumbing. So compared to that, being at sea was pretty good. Plus, that's where all the action is. He said once they even picked up a grizzly. It was swimming way out there, at least a mile from shore—who *knows* why?— anyway, it took four of them reaching out with gaff hooks, but they got him, and he was too exhausted to be pissed. The salmon were running, so they had tons aboard to feed him, but no one wants a grizzly on their boat, not for long. They weren't going to head back to Valdez, though, since that would mean giving up a full day's fishing. Instead they coaxed it into Greg's zodiac and had him pilot it ashore. He told me, "Sitting in a raft with a grizzly, that's something. Even with one who's got a reason to like you." And then he said this: "I still think about that bear now and then, start wondering what he's up to. You kind of remind me of him, that's probably part of it: swimming around lost, not knowing what you're searching for." Falling in love again and having a son, he thought that might help me. Greg's boy had just turned three that week, and standing on the dock—more aware of the wind than I had been, the sunlight making the lake look silver—it took a lot of work to think he wasn't right.

Dinner Date

"I guess it's their flapping," she told me. "It freaks me out. Even moths are kind of creepy. Whenever they get in, I let the cats eat them. Moths, I mean. But I'd let them loose on a bird if one flew in. Seagulls especially; they're the worst. And what are they doing here, anyway? Think about it: We're hundreds of miles from the ocean, but they're all over the place. You know how they got here? By following the freeway: Rest stop to rest stop, Burger King to Burger King, they just keep following the garbage. Like last week, I'm driving up State Street. I don't have AC in my car, so the windows are rolled down, and as I'm waiting for the light to change—I'm on the corner there by Carl's Jr.—the filthiest seagull I've ever seen dive-bombs this kid and snatches his fries. Only as it's flying off, another seagull attacks it, and they both land in the road and start hogging down fast as they can, hopping around in traffic. Well, the ugly one figures this isn't too smart, but it doesn't fly off in time. *Smack!* right off a windshield. And now it's flying all wobbly and sideways, into the street and up again all zigzag, straight through my window and into my lap, in my face, and I mean *I Am Screaming* and trying to shove it back out at the same time I'm trying not to touch it. And now the light turns green, and the car behind me keeps honking, and I've got this bird in the back seat, pecking at my head, flapping all over the place, and when I go to jump out, the door gets torn off by this Cadillac, and the woman—go figure, here she is in a *Cadillac*—doesn't have insurance. . . . Anyway, finally the cops show up, but what are they going to do, arrest it? put out an APB? I mean, it's a *seagull*. So I'm standing in the street, sobbing my eyes out, and I'm late for work, and the guy behind me is even more ticked off because he's late for some meeting and has to give his name and number as a witness. Then one of the cops and I hook up a couple weeks later—I know, I know, *what* was I thinking? Never date a cop—and of course that didn't work out.

Either he'd pout like a baby when I wouldn't wear his handcuffs, or he'd fly into a jealous rage whenever I went out, 'til one time he hauled off and hit me, and that was it. Of course, he wouldn't take no for an answer, and just try to get a restraining order on a cop, especially in Utah. So no," she told me and put down her menu, "I definitely don't want the chicken."

No Return Address

We'd driven down the coast on the 101 to this rugby tournament in Monterey. It's a great drive anyway without tequila, but we *did* have tequila, and lots of ice and beer, so even before we got to Eureka, the camaraderie had really kicked in: some combination of Dylan and AC/DC and Annie deciding, *she's* not waiting 'til we stop for gas; then she hung her butt out the window to pee while I hung on so she wouldn't fall. She didn't, of course. It's not that kind of story. Greg just stopped at the next town we came to, to hose down the side of the truck. He had this giant Chevy Suburban, and Annie had pretty much soaked it. That's what happens peeing in the wind. . . . Rugby's got little to do with this actually. I think we won a game or two, but I don't know; I can't remember. What I do remember is camping at Big Sur. If you've never been there, you should. You put up your tent, you're in a redwood forest. You get a fire going at night and watch the flames, you're in a redwood forest. You chug down aspirin and a ton of water so you won't be too hung over, *and you're in a redwood forest* with its green, and smells, and ocean cold, and air so clear it's like a telescope for the stars you find between the tops of trees as you're lying on your back in the moss and needles, and when you wake up in the morning, in the gray light and fog, that's right: You're waking up in a redwood forest. And if you're lucky like I was, you're going to go play rugby, and your coach already has a fire lit, and the coffee's boiling, and there are sausages, and he's stirring up a pot of baked beans. Now, I'd never had baked beans for breakfast, and I never have since, but I ate them then. *Man,* were they good. So was the coffee. We drank it black out of these dented, metal cups. And it's not like I'm some kind of Philistine. I've had lots of great food, I've got refined taste, and so on. But that morning there in the forest by the ocean, drinking coffee and eating baked beans, what can I say? You don't choose life off a menu. And what you'll always remember isn't always what you'd think.

"Well, it won't be funny when I explain it," Annie said, a month or so after we were married, "but you know how your imagination gets carried away, and then your conscious mind catches up, and you become aware of what you were thinking and how strange it is? I was thinking about how quiet it is tonight: like there's no one else in the world, and no world left except for this room. Like we're in a bomb shelter or something. And from there I started wondering if I *did* have to live in a bomb shelter, what would I take? And it wasn't the *Mona Lisa* or anything. I was thinking of tampons, actually. And how much water I'd need, and if I'd have enough to brush my teeth. And Carmex, too, 'cause I hate when my lips get dry. See what I mean? Who worries about toilet paper at the end of the world? It's crazy, really, 'cause if they ever *do* drop the bombs, then the *last* place I'll be is a fallout shelter. I'll be the one car headed in the wrong direction, cruising along with the top down, honking at everyone trying to escape and yelling, 'Good luck, suckers,' as I ride off into the flash point with a bottle of vodka and the stereo going full blast." . . . Then a minute or two passed, and her stomach rose and dropped and rose and dropped beneath my hand. Annie was sleeping. And her skin was warm. And suddenly the wind came gusting, bringing that cool, clean smell of the mountains, dancing open our bedroom curtains after three straight weeks of heat. I knew right then it would be raining soon and we'd wake up easy in the morning . . . just stay there together like we did and listen to the rain.

•

It was the weirdest thing I ever got in the mail. It was from Annie, ten years after our divorce, and it was her ashes. From being cremated. And there was this letter with them, all official, stating she'd donated her body for hospital research. She'd died— "Auto accident. DOA." —and they had this form she'd filled out when we were still married, naming me as next of kin. It was a strange feeling, believe me. Stranger than ghosts. First, you think it's a joke. Then you can't believe she's dead. Then you're finally left with wondering what to do. . . . So here's what I did. See, some things are more than an obligation, and I'd like to believe I got it right, just this one thing anyway. What I did was split her ashes into seven equal parts; it seemed like the right kind of number: mythic and lucky. The first part I took up to Mt. St. Helen's. It had been years since it blew up, but that's just seconds in geology, and that was the point: I figured she'd be there for the whole rebirth, that she'd be a part of it. From there I drove to Vantage, out on the bridge across the river, where the wind comes down the gorge at a hundred miles an hour. Her ashes flew everywhere, and I like to think they made it to the ocean . . . and Walla Walla . . . Puget Sound . . . and one day they'll wind up on a table in a restaurant where this couple is having some oysters, pasta, a bottle of wine, and right then he asks her to marry him, and she says yes, and it lasts forever. Then I kept on east to Polson, Montana, where the Rockies practically rise out of Flathead Lake. And the fourth part I went and scattered at Gasworks Park. You can see the whole Seattle skyline from there, and see the whole sky reflected in its glass. It's quite a place. And it's a quiet place. After that I went to Roy Street and left the fifth part in front of Bahn Thai. I love that restaurant. She'll get to smell that cooking every day. . . . For the sixth part, I had to go back to Spokane and scatter them over the falls. She always liked the Spokane River, especially there. It would've been her birthday. And that was that. It was all I could do at the time because the rest belonged in New Orleans. I needed to wait until Christmas, 'til the lights were up and shimmering on all the mansions and trees in the Garden District. It's amazing. Beautiful. Like what I think heaven will look like . . . assuming there really is one. And that we even need such a place.

IV

HOME APPRAISALS

Two-Story, Stone and Brick, Single-Family Dwelling

If there's added value in a ceiling fan,
then there must be value in a hawk. They come

for the doves, the ridiculous quail, and quick sparrows
squabbling daily on our neighbor's lawn,

suddenly plunging from nowhere, suddenly gone—
launched off before my eyes blink open.

And there must be value every time they miss
so *plunge* becomes *pursuit,* becomes a game

played out in fan-tailed figure-eights; it's wild:
your heartsong humming, the sky brighter blue. . . .

I know this won't go into the appraisal—
just bedrooms, baths, etc.; two-car garage.

There isn't any math that factors this.
No box to check if the front yard comes with a hawk.

Tool Shed, Workshop, Fully Fenced Backyard

Tomatoes can be yellow! Also small
and shaped like ovals! We're learning things here:

that leaving out a shovel equals rust,
that seeds and dirt can make food out of air,

that carrots follow their own thoughts underground—
they must, or why so many knots and curves

and none of them the same? We're learning sounds:
how August wind chimes mean a break from heat.

We're learning smells like *rain on dust*. It's too much
to count, to fit inside an estimate.

I'd measure me carrying the baby around
before I went in, verified square feet.

I'd measure me holding up things for him to touch,
saying *This is a pine cone, Jameson. This is a leaf.*

.17 Acres. Culinary Water

Not every decimal point is accurate.
They sometimes miss dimension, overlook

the sweep a peach tree adds to the backyard
just by moving in the wind. . . . Imagine it

gone now, downed by a storm. Imagine books
with missing pages . . . you know it's more than words

that disappear. So don't discount the tree.
There's more to calculate than area.

Last summer, for instance, in the kitchen—peaches peeled,
the crust rolled out—who knows what she saw,

exactly, as I stood there making pie?
But she flashed a smile as bright as cinnamon,

and I could tell *exactly* what she meant. . . .
Best one-point-something hours that whole July.

2,140 Square Feet

says nothing at all about the *un*square angles.
The living and dining rooms are heptagons — *amazing* —
I didn't even know that was a shape.

You pass between the two through an open arch
but not the kind of arch you see in church,
the kind you find in women: rounded hips,

the small of her back, her somersaulting laugh,
her slow smooth way of coming 'round from sleep.

Upstairs follows the roof line — trapezoids,
odd polygons. Three windows look out
at the mountains — more angles balancing the sky. . . .

Once when I was seventeen, the moon
looked close enough to walk to. Right there. Huge. . . .
The archway makes me think of that sometimes.

January 26, 2009

Forty-three thousand job cuts in one day,
in just one morning. Thirty thousand more

by late-afternoon. Mine wasn't one of them.
We're not part of the millions since last May

who've lost their homes—lost porches and front doors,
the mantel 'round their fireplace, the trim

they painted 'round the windows one April:
pale green to go with her flower garden.

Or the place where he first saw her naked.
Or their kids' favorite hiding closet. All . . .

whatever the details, whatever their plans. . . .
How do you fit that in boxes, tape-gun it shut?

I don't know; the news didn't answer. Instead they ran
the weather: *Cold.* Then a story about a duck.

3 Bdrm, 2 Ba, Kitchen, Frml Dining

The baby has a bed but likes ours more.
He lets us know it, too. He lets it fly:

like crossing two cats fighting with a war
between accordions. *But he is cute,* for sure.

And he'd eat everything if he had teeth,
eat all the foods his sister won't: the fruit,

the eggplant parmesan, whatever's there;
already he's reaching like a quick-draw artist.

And here is where he'll learn to walk, then run,
then go out back in our sun-fat garden—

Yes, the house has a crawl space underneath.
Yes, the radiator's certified—

I'm picturing him with his brothers and sister:
all that noisy tangle in the yard.

Upgrades to the Property: <u>N/A</u>

So none of what I'm telling you applies;
it's all *not applicable.* I'm not surprised;

it's just another headline like the rest:
like *Economic Crisis Faces Pres.,*

like *More Firms Pressed to Liquidate,*
like *Home Sales Sluggish, Price Decay,* that's all.

My cat, for one, could care less. He's focused
on squirrels: right up the tree trunks, onto limbs.

He's pretty bad-ass. He'd stretch out on the news,
or credit report and appraisal, and go to sleep . . .

I think that's worth a note or two, don't you?
And the grape vines, hawks, the backyard corner

where the swing-chair hides behind camellias?
And how, when it's still, you can hear the whole house purr?

When I Asked My Friend the Entomologist,

Processional

"Is it true . . . does a female praying mantis kill its mate
by biting its head off?" she said, "Sure,

but at least they're honest about it.
And they get it done with faster than a woman."

She's pretty thin herself,
wears toughness like an exoskeleton,

but I've seen her run across a football field behind a moth
just because they're beautiful,

because you don't see many in the daytime,
and she'll buy herself a dress for New Year's Eve—

one year it was monarch orange,
another it was dragonfly blue, knee-length,

dramatically backless.
She said it was a kind of camouflage,

that she had to blend in with the champagne bubbles.
"But yeah," she admitted, "I'm hoping for some of that too."

Arrival

When I asked what she meant about women,
she didn't explain. My yard was more interesting:

A baby bird had fallen out of its nest,
and my cat had killed it and set it on a rock—

a nice flat one, almost like a dinner plate—
and I wanted to know what was eating it, hornets or bees?

She could have answered on the phone, of course,
but figured she might as well come on over.

The bees were gone by the time she got here . . .
just ants, a fly, doing clean-up work inside the rib cage.

She said, "It doesn't take a scientist to be an observer.
You've spent some time around women; you tell me."

Burial

It's been a good summer for bumble bees.
Something about the weather:

rain in April, and for once
an unscorched June.

Last month, one of them was different though.
It had a bright red circle on its abdomen.

"Probably *Bombus centralis*," she told me,
"as common in Utah as dandelions."

But then, since I'd come all the way to her lab,
she said, "Unless . . .".

I've always like that word—like a lighthouse
keeping an eye on possibility.

I tend to forget that a lighthouse is signaling risk.
"Unless it's *sylvicola*.

They typically stick to Montana, Wyoming,
parts of Colorado.

They're rare around here,
but sometimes they'll surprise."

She picked up a marker,
lifted her T-shirt,

drew a bright red circle on her stomach.
She said, *"Bombus centralis* or *sylvicola,* which am I?"

Recessional

A praying mantis would have answered her
and had it add up to a story.

A bee would have flown with that invitation to the hive.
There would have been honey.

I guess that's the upside of instinct:
You know what to do.

I stand on the porch some nights
and listen to the unison crickets,

or maybe my cat brings a hummingbird moth in the house
and the chase goes from windows

to light bulbs.
Some days I look at those bird bones

and hope she comes around.
I've heard there are ants so strong

they can carry away a person's anger.
I want to ask my friend the entomologist if that's true.

The Fisherman Knew It Was a Strange Arrangement:

You can't catch fish in the house.
Even if he ran a river down the hallway

or poured a small ocean in the living room . . .
maybe buried the couch under sand dunes,

it wouldn't be the same. The curtains would never be seagulls.
Her closet would never be the woods.

A few nights a year, once the house was sleeping,
he'd stay up late and remember.

He'd open the faucets
just to hear the water say its name.

And sometimes he'd even feel a strike—
that live tugging—

like the nerves in his arms swam directly to his heart,
like his guts still knew where they came from

before all this. . . .
In the morning, he'd wake with his limit on the stringer:

the image of rainbow trout for his breakfast,
the memory of salmon for his lunch.

When They'd Gotten the Bear in the Cage,

it was punished for their anger,
for taking up space where they would've preferred potted plants

or a pretty aquarium: a shimmer of fish
like the room's own rainbow,

and bubbles coming from a deep-sea diver,
and there on the glass their own faces smiling back.

It was punished whenever a growl escaped.
Then threatened with worse for its silence.

The next morning, they hammered up signs all around it:
No quiet unhappiness allowed.

They hung banners demanding that it laugh more,
colored pie charts of all of its problems,

threw sticks in its cage and told it to go fetch,
which all makes perfect sense

if you twist sense like a corkscrew
and the only wine you ever open is the bottle of your own desire.

A Lesson Every Shipwreck Learns Too Late

Boats don't know they're boats.
That's why they can float on the water.

If they knew their anchors weren't house keys,
knew the waves weren't their own steady heartbeats . . .

if they knew their sails were only sails
and not them breathing out and in . . .

they'd nosedive down, plunge
suddenly as pocket change

somebody dropped. They'd lie there broken
on the living room floor.

Years from now you could visit them,
put on a wetsuit and air tank,

explore among fish
and the coral kaleidoscopes,

the here-and-gone shadows of sharks,
but what do you think you'd find?

That sunken trawler was no treasure boat.
That passenger ferry was a passenger ferry.

Even you, my sloop, you're ordinary:
sailing along toward your no less ordinary loss.

The Two of Them Are Hard to Tell Apart

One morning, the man felt his shadow wake up early,
heard it open the closet and put on the shadows of his clothes.

While he lay there—still, and listening—his shadow
set the water on for coffee,

then it went outside
and raked the shadows of leaves into piles.

When it stopped to smoke,
he smelled the shadow of a cigarette.

And later, as it read the paper,
he could follow the shadows of the news:

no mention of him and his strange separation . . .
no stories covering an earthquake or eclipse . . .

if he wanted an answer, the man was on his own.
And so he observed, he followed after,

he shadowed his shadow through winter into spring,
watched it planting some hyacinth beans,

watched it rigging a trellis of shadows to his fence.
Like maybe those vines would make a difference.

Like someone might see him near his shadow
and know which one was which.

Of All the Gifts She Ever Gave Him—

the empty lake, the static on the radio, the years
with missing handle bars—

the one that halfway fit him was the gloves.
He wore them all spring, then all summer, weeding

even by moonlight, relentless as a ghost,
as constant as the sky we ignore

'til geese fly south and give us a reason to look:
their sad, odd honking like the sound of our desire. . . .

Of course, he was crazy;
all the couples on our street know that.

One morning we woke to the noise of him weeding
his house, uprooting the plumbing, uprooting

every lost night from their bed. Yanking
light bulbs. Yanking telephones. Miles of red wire.

And I almost admire his fierce logic,
though I know enough to keep it to myself:

Finally he reached in the mirror, pulled
hard, and disappeared.

Sometimes It Isn't the Same Old Story

You could understand him misunderstanding,
digging such careful holes with his shovel,

sifting in spoonfuls of birdseed—
an honest mistake.

And you could half-understand how he stubbornly finished,
how he aimed his back at everyone laughing

and patted the dirt down
gently with his hands.

But to greet each day with his watering can,
to go on as if he were a gardener, as if he *believed* . . .

someone finally stomped all the green in his yard,
and that should've been the end of that.

Certainty feels like a flag when you fly it. It snaps in the wind
and makes the sound of your own good name,

of your own high opinion. It's the opposite of birds.
And it was birds that he was growing, after all:

cardinals, robins, chickadees, starlings.
His seedlings stood up again,

unfurled their branches,
all of them loaded not with blossoms but with song.

That was the season people re-learned amazement,
followed by the autumn when they re-learned amazement again:

One morning he went 'round his yard on a ladder.
He paid no attention to everyone clapping,

just picked each bird and released it into the sky.

V

ARRIVALS

In the Only Zombie Flick I'll Watch,

Processional

it isn't brains they're after.
It's our phones—

our iPhones and smart phones,
all our zillion juicy JPEGs—

so when the splatter starts,
blood won't geyser onto lawns, intestines

won't tangle in a rose bush.
There won't be cinematic, slo-mo close-ups of wet red

dripping from the leaves.
No bone-cracks splintered by surround sound

or eyeballs popping like gory corks,
just mangled metal, plastic bits, and naked wire . . .

phones stalked and surrounded
and screaming on the swung ends of charger cords

again, and again, and again
against brick walls.

Hold on to your catharsis, people,
the zombies are coming to eat you where it hurts,

Arrival

though of course this is metaphor.
It says so on every syllabus.

It's generic Defense of the Genre 101:
our anxieties projected,

the dead-alive virus of consumerism,
suburban fear of wild animals

whose wildness is safely on TV,
and so on, and so on. Take your pick.

I'm picking Righteous Havoc;
in *The Only Zombie Flick I'll Watch*, they're here

to lash back: Genetically-modified watermelons
made square for easier stacking? Attack!

Mountain Dew ad men asking,
"Are you dissatisfied with your morning-beverage options?" —

slug down another mug of coffee,
blend a pomegranate smoothie,

drink a glass of ordinary orange juice,
and attack! Reach into their servers

and rip out the heart, or chip,
or whatever you call it. Attack.

Burial

Don't worry, they're actors.
And they'd probably all prefer a different role.

One played a genie in an indie film . . .
aired April 8th on the Sundance Channel, 4 a.m.

It didn't pay, but she liked the writing,
liked the wishes of the boy who found her:

"First, turn the guns into hunting falcons.
Then all the bullets into pheasants.

And third, let nobody use this wish
so they can't make any mistakes with it."

When they'd wrapped, after they'd struck the set,
the cast and crew went for Udon noodles,

and the view of the harbor out the window
never looked so clean.

Even now, typecast as a Zombie Prom Queen
grinding her tiara in a redneck's bluetooth,

there's an unspent wish inside her
safe from idiocy and greed.

Recessional

So we've come to the dénouement,
where the zombies are bored with their mayhem.

A few stragglers chase a blonde
in a storm-soaked nightgown,

another gnaws on an iPad,
but they're done. The spirit's gone out of it,

and they lack an articulate spokesman,
a leader to formulate a slogan

they can text
or silkscreen on T-shirts,

maybe hang around wearing them at concerts or something
and stream the whole thing live.

Yeah, that would be easier.
Go home and watch it all on YouTube.

Sit there staring at the new tribal fire
while the final credits roll.

ACKNOWLEDGMENTS

Thank you to the editors of the following journals in which these poems, or earlier versions, sometimes under different titles, first appeared:

Bateau 3.2 (2010): "Lost and Found."

Cave Wall 11 (2012): "Break a Leg, and They Put You Out to Pasture."

ellipsis . . . literature & art 50 (2014): "When I Asked My Friend the Entomologist."

Harpur Palate 10.1 (2010): "When They'd Gotten the Bear in the Cage."

Hothouse Magazine (6 April 2014): "To the Man Who Scored 300k to Cry Wolf Before Congress on Behalf of Utah, a State in Which There Are No Wolves."

Kestrel 25 (2010): "The Church of the Stars and the Moon."

LitRag 8 (2000): "What I Would Take" (the middle section of "No Return Address").

LitRag 6 (1999): "Dinner Date."

The MacGuffin 17.2 (2000): "No Return Address" (the final section of the poem).

Mobius: The Journal of Social Change 23.3 (2012): "Here in What Used to Be Mexico."

Poecology 4 (2014): "Every Place I've Ever Lived Is Gone."

Redactions: Poetry, Poetics, & Prose 17 (2013): "To the Representative on the House Science, Space, and Technology Committee, Who in 2012 Said, 'Evolution, Big Bang Theory, All That Is Lies Straight from the Pit of Hell,' I Offer This Quick Study on Natural Selection, in Which the Eagle Is Thought; the River Is Reason; the Salmon Is Insight; Tomorrow Is a Salmon; and the Crows, of Course, Are You."

Redactions: Poetry & Poetics 12 (2009): "Sometimes It Isn't the Same Old Story."

River Styx 76/77 (2008): "Monterey Invitational" (the opening section of "No Return Address").

Santa Fe Literary Review (2009): "Undercurrents."

Sugar House Review 5.2 (2013): "In the Only Zombie Flick I'll Watch"; "To the Woman at the Conference on Writing for Social Change Who Asked, 'What Was Your Upbringing? What Were Your Parents Like? How Did You Get This Open-Minded?' . . . I Don't Remember My Answer but Wish I'd Said This:"

Sugar House Review 4.2 (Fall/Winter 2012): "A Lesson Every Shipwreck Learns Too Late"; "The Two of Them Are Hard to Tell Apart."

Sugar House Review 2 (Fall/Winter 2010): "Two-Story, Stone and Brick, Single-Family Dwelling"; "Tool Shed, Workshop, Fully Fenced Backyard"; ".17 Acres. Culinary Water"; "2,140 Square Feet"; "January 26, 2009"; "3 Bdrm, 2 Ba, Kitchen, Frml Dining"; "Upgrades to the Property: N/A" under the title "Home Appraisals."

Terrain.org: A Journal of the Built & Natural Environments 30 (2012): "Suggestions for Urban Renewal"; "To the Man in the Jaunty Golf Cap, Wow."

Terrain.org: A Journal of the Built & Natural Environments 28 (2011): "Eagle Ridge, Eagle Crest, Eagle View"; "Here in the Rugged, Noble West"; "If Wolves Lope into Your Dreams."

Weber — The Contemporary West 28.1 (2011): "88 Maps"; "The Fisherman Knew It Was a Strange Arrangement."

"Two-Story, Stone and Brick, Single-Family Dwelling" and "January 26, 2009" were included in *New Poets of the American West*. Ed. Lowell Jaeger. Kalispell, MT: Many Voices Press, 2010.

The following appeared in the chapbook *Home Appraisals* (Plan B Press, 2012):

"88 Maps," "A Lesson Every Shipwreck Learns Too Late," "Break a Leg, and They Put You Out to Pasture," "Home Appraisals," "Of All the Gifts She Ever Gave Him," "Sometimes It Isn't the Same Old Story," "The Church of the Stars and the Moon," "The Fisherman Knew It Was a Strange Arrangement," "The Two of Them Are Hard to Tell Apart," and "When They'd Gotten the Bear in the Cage."